A Moon Shadow Nocturne

Table of Contents

Rachel Lawson

As written on website AllPoetry.com http://allpoetry/The_Poette
Cover made with Canva
Copyright 2021 Rachel Lawson

All Rights Reserved
No part of this book may be reproduced, or performed,
stored in retrieval systems or transmitted in any form
by electronic, mechanical, photocopying, recording means
or otherwise without prior written permission by author
contact author via website
https://rachellawsonpoet.yolasite.com/

A Moon Shadow Nocturne

A play of light and dark,
under the wan light of the moon plays with the skipping shadows of
night's dance their bewitching saraband with the moonlight,
silver moonlight and darkness melt into one in the cool airs of the
nocturnal bower of night,
the stars sparkle in the shadows far above the worldly cradle of man,
it is pure enchantment by moonlight,
a nocturne of moonlight and shadows melding it to one,
a song both dark and light with an ethereal heady air of enchantment
leaving the heart aglow

Why Do We Write Poetry?

Poetry has a magic all its own,
in the mind, the seed is sown,
from the pen, pretty words flow out,
to be read by the devout,
the words seem smoother than honey,
the words worth are more than money,
without poetry, there is nothing but despair,
poetry is beyond compare.

The Marvelous Light

Crystalline pure silvery aura of night,
is within my sight,
the moon glows full and bright,
it is a marvelous light.

Riding the waves of time

I ride the waves of time,
I live in the past, present, and future for a while,
I know what has come to be,
I know not what will come to be,
I know the past like an old friend,
I ride through the present upon the wake of the past to the future,
I was born in the past and will die in the future one grave day,

Breaking through the wall

Going beyond hitting the wall,
Is hard not too not only for me but all,
It's like banging your head into a brick wall,
Your stamina and strength are lost none left to recall,
You cannot go on you are left fearing you may fall,
You need the cool chilling healing balm of rest for it to stall,
But you must go on beyond the wall,
You cannot stop until you breach that wall.

Like a Moth to a Flame

Humans chase the sun like a moth to a flame,
we rise with the sun and hibernated when the sun leaves,
We adore her sister the moon who is lit by the sun's loving glow,
The sun warms our hearts in our Earthly bower.

When We Were Young

When we were young the world was magical,
When we were young we were immortal,
When we were young the world was ours,
When we were young we could do anything,
When we were young our dream would all come true,
When we were young nothing could stop us,
When we were young love would find us,
When we were young anything was possible,
When we were young the world was a dream,
When we were young the world was our pearl,
When we were young fantasy was real,
When we were young we were all swashbuckling heroes,
When we were young no one could stop us,
When we were young we were dreamers,
When we were young romance was real,
When we were young there was always a happy ending.

In My Life

I have lived a life in dreams,
not all is as it seems,
everything is running as theme,
it's a lovely dream,
melting into a pool of happiness and pain,
like a bittersweet refrain,
sang by a melancholy singer in a song so sweet,
I know the future I will meet,
with similar heartfelt empathy as I do the past,
all comes and goes until days last.

A thousand million eyes

They say the night has a thousand eyes,
That "One could not count the moons that shimmer on her roofs, or the
thousand splendid suns that hide behind her wall."
Beautiful sparkling eyes of stars the lonely travelers of the skies,
thy light charms all,
thy fires eternally burn,
the silvery beams from moons and suns illuminate the night with night's
alluring glow
the light of these hundred million suns and moons illuminate lovers
perpetual yearn,
they are distant and far memories of days eons ago.

The Eyes of Night

They say the night has a thousand eyes,
not many know the hows or whys,
they are the stars of light,
they are a beautiful sight,
they are the burning embers of stars long past,
they are the eyes of the night to their last,
when they close their eyes in fire or ice,
till their ends, someone always says it nice

By Candlelight

I read lonely by dim candlelight,
late it is at the night,
the room is scarcely encompassed by the candle's wan glow,
I dream of the new miracle light electric bulb it would Illuminate the
darkness as I know,
I curse the dull light of the candle as I can't see to read with it,
with a light bulb, the night's dark aura will submit,
to become like the light of midday,
not the of night pale and dark but with a bulb night's blindness is kept
at bay.

Requiem

Under the moon's silver glow,
I could forget everything and live in this moment forever,
tugs on the heartstrings like a beautiful voice in song,
words are the dreams the heart makes,
all now of the dream I have is a requiem.

When The Mirror Cracked

Due to circumstances beyond my control,
the mirror cracked when the bell did toll,
with that, all went wrong,
everything went in flames lifelong,
it felt like ice flowing through my veins,
all I did was in vain me it pains,
it was like fishing without bait,
I tried fixing the mirror but it was too late,
bad luck was all I caught,
I never reached what I sought,
my horse broke its legs,
I dropped a basket of eggs,
milk I spilled,
my dream remains unfulfilled,
misery I feel,
I feel I am trying to hold a slippery eel,
the sharks ate my fish,
I am squeamish,
nothing is going right,
hope is out of sight.

Requiem For a Dream 2

I lament awaking from my dream sublime,
but all sleepers will wake in time,
I feel lost and alone without my dream,
I feel I am missing a vital seam,
I am like a tree broken at the stem,
all now of the dream I have is a requiem.

The Wind Chime

Ting, tink, ting
ting, tink, ting,
the little chimes do sing,
the breeze trough it gently blows,
how long they will ring who knows,
when the wind goes

Edgar Allan Poe

Darkness within darkness,
lightness within lightness,
perfection and precision,
the night's clarion,
and the heart's musician,
a great master of the poetic composition,
love in words of beauty,
beauty in a Raven's duty,
barer of a dark raven's heart,
grim words for those dark of heart,
echo like a dream like nightmare in the mind,
his words ring through the spirit of mankind
all the way through future times.
know as master of prose and rhymes
from the first time I heard of his raven I've been haunted by the words
he bore,
nevermore shall be heard in my dark soul evermore.

Haiku By Coup

The haiku form makes no sense to me,
There be neither rhyme nor reason in a haiku to be,
Haiku are maths cross poetry they only confuse,
Mathes and poetry don't well mix that is why to do haiku I refuse.

Yellow

I dream a dream so clear and mellow,
a soft sun glowing bright and yellow.
illuminating dawn dark and new,
the golden sun peeking out beneath the blue,
thick as golden honey,
smooth as fine held sand leaking from a hand runny,
the shadows drown in the sun's warm glow,
the world begins to Itself show.

as old parchments do the sands of the shores of dawn glow,
the daylight grows longer ever so slow,
like molten gold, the sky the day wakes up brighter,
chasing away the yellow stars of the night as it starts growing lighter,
the day has come bright as a morning can be,
the sky is blue and clear all can see,
the golden sun beats down warming heart and soul it did evoke
and then bathed in the light of the golden morn I awoke.

The Sea of Blue

I see a sea of blue,
a floral ocean of a single hue,
beneath a sky azure painted with fluffy clouds,
I am alone and breathless in these crowds,
the flowers are like water hugging the ground,
ever so enchanting blue above and blue, below blue all around,
I am drowning in this sea of blue,
it is the most intoxicating brew,
I drink in with my eyes this beauty,
I am light and heady,
I'm in heaven on Earth,
the beauty is beyond worth,
it is like a sea of cut aquamarine,
the sky is blue cloudy turquoise, no bluest tourmaline,
oh my, it is so enchanting I can barely speak,
I can not find more words I am speechless and I feel weak.

Liquid Gold

smoother than honey,
like a golden sunset sunny,
rich as glowing golden honey,
thick and runny
worth more than money.

Silver

Shiny metal of liquid white,
attractive and light,
natures gift to man,
posses it if you can,
it possesses you,
you, it does subdue.

Breath is life

Life with out breath is death,
I will breathe till my day of my death,
breath is the life of a man,
no breath his death.

Death's Token

Upon my grave do not grieve,
Just leave upon it death's token in reprieve,
A single lily fear not my grave be not chilly,
It is the home of love I am now in heaven far above.

New Ways To Dream

I dream and see any thing can be,
It is a new way to dream for me,
I dream I can do anything,
I am so happy I feel like I can sing,
I could dance I feel high,
People ask me why?
I know my dream to them impossible does seem,
But I have found new ways to dream.

Moonlight on the Water

A sparkling river cool and clear,
enchanted by nature's beauty divine,
pure elegance to the eye and mind.

In The Moonlight Hour

Stillness,
silence,
a cool air,
a silvery glow all around,
pure beauty,
darkness cut by moonlight and starlight.

Thoughts

Life and death all come and go slow and fast,
sad and happy they are,
things come and go,
where will I go? When will I come?

The Night Is Like A Beautiful Gem

The stars are silver sparkling gems floating in the onyx sea of pitch,
the moon like an illuminated glowing gem moonstone that swims
through the starlit sky,
the air is cool and misty upon the lake tonight,
the ground sparkles with its frosty carpet,
the night is like a beautiful gem tonight.

Vampire love

Your blood is my blood,
my blood is your blood,
like my heart is yours,
and your heart is mine,
you are my love,
I am your love,
we are one.

Dreaming

A fantasy world is dreaming,
beyond wakeful deeming,
nothing is as it should be,
nothing is beyond what you can see,
floating through the air,
without a worry or care,
that is all in a dream,
nothing is what it may seem.

The Blue Rose of Egypt

The blue lotus of the Nile,
it is a beauty there is no denial,
drug of the ancients,
its flower bloom requires patience,
it blooms but one time only,
the rose of Egypt bloom is lonely.

Under the dust of the past lie, the days gone by

Under the dust of the past lie, the days gone by
lost in the shadows of time is where the dreams of the past do die,
from the night comes the new days to come,
it is from the dust the grows the world as it will become.

The Dark Side of the Hourglass

The sands in the hourglass creep by briskly,
with the sands fall lives and times and eras,
swift death comes when the sands of life's glass flow of sand stops,
it brings ends to lives, times and all thing within their sands stream draw
to it's end.

The Eternal Flame

I burn with hope like an eternal flame,
the flame ignites a burning bright light,
I see things that never have been seen before,
the fire crackles and illuminates the mind,
the light awakens the soul to new things.

The Sea Horse

Beauty of the sea,
both horse and fish,
hippocampus, Horse of the seas,
swims and shimmers like a fish,
Poseidon's chariot steed

The Surgeon

This church is in my blood,
My bones and my ancestors lie in this church,
In life, I fixed man's flesh and bones,
I was the father of many men of medicine,
some of my children traveled to distant lands,
I was a Victorian man of my time,
I lie in death with my children and relatives long gone.
I lie where pilgrims traverse to see where Shakespeare once lay.
Including one of the young future mothers of my descendants to come.

Requiem for a Dream

I grieve the loss of a dream,
I feel like from me tore a seam,
I lost my faith and hope with it,
I am lost sad and lonely I admit,
I fear life without the dream I bore,
I was happy in the light of my dream before,
I feel my dream has died,
I feel it to me had lied.
will you my dream just fade away,
disappear in an echo of pain one day as dreams do decay.

The Reign of Rain

Cool and softly falls the rain,
from the silvery sky,
it comes sweetly hissing on my roof,
refreshing the world with its life-giving nectar.

Saturn

Rings and diamonds,
a precious gem of space,
planet of ice and rock,
pressure under beauty,
diamonds melting into crystalline liquid diamonds in death.

Ghost Light

By ghost light, the lonely stage is lit,
no one is there it is lit for ghosts alone,
all of the actors are hiding from the stage,
people in crowds are shunned,
the era is one of fear,
so no one even there comes near,
only the ghost of productions past are there.

Time Travel

I am a time traveler, as are we all, we travel through time moment by moment, the possibility of time and chance are considered possible in parallel universes, we all live on in this universal life, balancing upon the tightrope which is time and choice, controlling in which parallel world within which we live and die.

The Rain Falls

I watch as the rain falls,
I here as it calls,
on my tin roof, it hisses,
in calming whispers.
it washes the heat from the air,
the summer heat cools to a temperature easier to bear.

The Mystery of Night

They say the night has a thousand Eyes,
It's beauty no one denies,
The nocturnal passing is cool and crisp,
The mind creates ghosts from a single wisp,
No man knows night truly,
Man knows it comes by dark and cooly,
It has a feeling of enchantment,
Beholders are usually lost in the moment,
The glazed eye that is the moon comes ever slowly,
In the dark speckled sky, people watch them longingly,
As they float by in night's procession,
They travel by with great precision,
Til wthe dawn time chorus comes,
And the day It becomes.

Let it snow

Softly falls the snow,
making hearts aglow,
cool crisp,
floating in a wisp.

Wildflowers

Common some call them,
I am charmed by their wild exotic beauty,
they are to me dear to my heart,
they are elegant delicate beauties of nature,
although some call them weed,
but one man's weed is another's flower,
a dog rose is still a rose,
a wild bluebell still a beauty,
an onion weed still is sweet to the eye,
a flower is still a flower no-matter what you call it.

The Rose of Snow

Once existed a pure white rose,
from the snow, it rose,
a rose of purest snow,
from the snow, it did grow,
and by the snow, it did die,
in death, it was petals in the snow it did lie.

O, Woe is me

O, Woe is me I am but fate's toy,
I am without joy,
I am a merely fates pawn I maltreated and expendable,
my doom is the only thing I know is the only thing dependable,
I live but for a whim of fate,
I am resigned to my state.

Sky Diamonds

Diamonds made of air,
Too precious to share,
Diamonds made by man,
Made only as scientists and dreamers can.

Dick Turpin and the King of the Road

Upon the road, the King, Tom, met Turpin,
Turpin thought King was a fat pigeon,
they rode together on their way,
the robbed people with their guns under the code of the men of the
highway,
"The money or your life?" they did call,
it was nothing or all,
Tom made Turpin a highwayman legend,
it was rumored Turpin brought King's end,
Tom was shot in the shoulder,
he was taken to the Doctor,
he could not be saved,
Turpin, goodbye to the road he waved,
a butcher he became,
he was caught under a charge of poaching claim,
he wrote a letter for help from one of his in-laws,
the only problem was the letter his death's cause,
an old teacher of Turpin's read through his identity fraud,
they knew his handwriting he told truth and not no one could save him
not even the good Lord.
he was revealed and caught,
the gallows called according to the court.
death came swiftly,
the legend grew greater hereby.

The Song of the Wheat Field

I stand amid a golden wheat field,
the wind blows the wheat which bends and folds,
so sweetly waving,
the breeze blowing through the wheat,
makes the wheat start to sing.
it sings long sad arias like mournful sighs.

A Nodding field of Crocuses

I stand in a field of Autumn Crocuses,
bobbing in the strong autumn wind,
I see a few grasshoppers or were they locusts,
whatever it is it is just in the viewer's mind.

The air is of silver and pearl, the night is liquid with moonlight- extended

The stars are silver diamonds placed upon a black velvet sky,
the leaves in the wind are gems floating in the cool crisp air,
the rain is falling stars like glowing diamonds,
the river is crystalline rippling mercury beneath the full moon's light,
the night is full of the sounds of life,
crickets chirp, frogs croak, night birds sing their sweet serenade of night,
my boat cuts through the river with a soft swish of water,
an ethereal glowing fog is hiding the river in patches,
the air is full of the scents of flowers on the shore,
the moon is like the gem moonstone bright and clear peaking out of the
clouds are shadowy faintly glowing cotton candy mist,
"The air is of silver and pearl, the night is liquid with moonlight."
I am breathless.

The Coming of Winter

Autumn has fallen,
winter is callin'
I feel the cold breath of winter blowing through me to the bone,
the leaves have all fell the clear blue skies of Fall have gone,
the sky is cloudy the days are growing wet,
I know it is coming soon to winters lowering sunset,
the yule tide cometh soon bringing with it white snow,
with snowmen, Christmas trees and hearts aglow,
the lighter side of this bleak season,
it is a magical ethereal time of beauty I love it for that reason.

Who Wants To Live Forever

Who wants to live forever,
who wants to die never,
who wants their world to never end in fatality,
who could take immortality?
who could stay sane,
who could take the pain,
who could take the loss of all they love,
who could but dream of heaven above,
who could take the aeons in their stride,
who could just sit and take the eternal ride,
who could not go mad,
who could not be sad,
who would want to see life wane,
who could have hope seeing the fade of life's chain,
who would go on smiling boldly,
who would not end up acting coldly,
Who wants to live forever,
who wants to die never,
who wants their world to never end in fatality,
who could take immortality?

Dreams

Words are the dreams the heart makes,
They are the wishes of the mind,
They are the heartaches and sighs,
They are the breaths and cries,
They are the life and end,
The light and dark,
They are the beauty of the night,
The warmth of the day,
The visions of the heart made real.

Dusk To Dawn

The eventide brings with it the coldest hours
the daylight the night devours,
cold and wan the light does grow,
the sun goes to its roost leaving in her place the moon and stars aglow,
in her silvery bower,
the moon rules the night it is her hour,
when the dawn comes to the silver realm,
the night is no longer at the helm,
the night burns away,
into the golden light of day.

Water Color

Upon a lake swam 2 perfect snow-white birds,
the scene in whole was beyond words,
the water was stained with the colors of the autumnal trees nearby,
like a rainbow of color, the trees seemed to reach to the sky,
the dear little swans appeared oblivious to the beauty,
they swam about as if it was their duty.

Moon Rise

The moon rises from a dark burning sea,
ink black clouds like smoke float between it and me,
the land is as dark as the night sky,
the clouds like smoke over the fiery water float by.

There is No Comeback From This

like glass smashed I am shattered,
like sand by the wind scattered,
I am like the last of my kind in an a world alone,
heartbroken I am left to bemoan,
the world has fallen apart,
I am down in heart.

Stardust- the children of the Stars

We are stardust the children of the stars,
the stars are our ancestors,
the elements of our bodies come from this,
as with the soul, the mind, the egos,
we are but living and thinking stardust,
star children who must search for more to be best,
are we alone or have we family in space,
we who forget we are of one race,
the children of the stars,
our brothers and sisters are planets like Earth and Mars.

The Sea of Blue

I see a sea of blue,
a floral ocean of a single hue,
beneath a sky azure painted with fluffy clouds,
I am alone and breathless in these crowds,
the flowers are like water hugging the ground,
ever so enchanting blue above and blue, below blue all around,
I am drowning in this sea of blue,
it is the most intoxicating brew,
I drink in with my eyes this beauty,
I am light and heady,
I'm in heaven on Earth,
the beauty is beyond worth,
it is like a sea of cut aquamarine,
the sky is blue cloudy turquoise, no bluest tourmaline,
oh my, it is so enchanting I can barely speak,
I can not find more words I am speechless and I feel weak.

Kitty and the Yule Log

Kitty loves to be warm,
she sits by the fire away from the storm,
kitty is cutely sitting near a log of the yule tide as it does burn,
for the heat of the hearth she does yearn.

Dust of Eternity

The past is the dust of eternity,
it draws out all of memory,
it is the shadow of known time,
the sands of the hourglass fallen,
long is time on reverse looking back,
beyond the sands fallen is the future,
the sands waiting to fall.

Byronesque

She lifts the clouds, like the night
Of cloudless climes and starry skies;
She lifts them out of sight
For her time flies;
Beyond the day to night
And what is beyond she spies.

Distruzione di Rhapsody (Rhapsody of Destruction) 2

I am an artist,
I play violins,
with a sword.

Reflections of Night

Sparkling jewels upon the water,
Come to my feverish mind,
Ethereal and Enchanting like a lovers song,
Heady yet delicate like a mist at sea,
Glowing like my arduous heart,
A sight never to be forgot,
Lighting the night with their faint iridescence,
Dying with the dawn's light.

The Dark Mystery of Night

It is a play of light and dark,
illuminated by a silvery spark,
what lies hidden out of sight,
it is the dark mystery which is the night.

Tigers in the Snow

My heart is wild and free like tigers in the snow,
it loves to run far and free when it is my heart is all aglow,
to dream to live and run forever on wards,
though I look backwards,
and see where I have been to learn from the past,
as I go ever forward until my days last.

Dance of the Grinches

Bah Humbug! It's Christmas time,
When sensible people lose all their money it's winter time,
hate winter the ice and snow,
the houses a glow,
The no parking,
the people sing,
The traffic jams
the hams,
the empty stores,
the wreaths on doors.

Words have no power to impress the mind without the exquisite horror of their reality.

Darkness within darkness,
lightness within the night,
the pale wan light from the moon,
cuts through the dark of night,
things hidden in the dark are-
illuminated by fair Luna's light,
they are brought into sight,
a door is opened into another world,
the world of night is revealed,
thus the unseen world is now within sight.

Fire in the Sky

Like liquid white fire was the meteoric deluge,
like falling starlight on the starry night sky,
like glowing rain falling through the dark sky,
enchanting the heart and mind charming the very soul,
with every falling star.

Castles in the sky

Nothing is what it seems,
nothing is what the dreamer dreams,
they dream of lands a far,
they are never what they think they are,
they are just castles in the sky,
but for their dream the dreamer see pure and perfect place but if they go
there the dream would die.

THE END

Don't miss out!

Visit the website below and you can sign up to receive emails whenever Rachel Lawson publishes a new book. There's no charge and no obligation.

https://books2read.com/r/B-A-HMGO-LGOTB

BOOKS 2 READ

Connecting independent readers to independent writers.

Also by Rachel Lawson

Poetry
Night Poetry
Requiem for a Dream
A Moon Shadow Nocturne

Stand and Deliver
In The Moonlight

The Magicians
The Mask Magician and other stories

Watch for more at https://rachellawsonpoet.yolasite.com/.

About the Author

Rachel is a lover of gothic poetry and the stories of Emilly Dickensen, Poe, and other poets and writers. she writes in a gothic sometimes romantic, and somewhat eclectic style. She likes to do a good job in whatever she does, and she tried her hand from amateur Magic to designing objects for 3d printing. She has loved writing since primary school at high school she wrote plays and wrote short stories and made her essays look like books she has been in training for quite a while. She first wrote about the magicians in her teens. She devised Stand and Deliver: In The Moonlight in her 20's as a short story and re-wrote the story in her 40's. She wrote poetry and story into her 20's and took a break from writing for a few years while she helped out as a stage assistant in a local theatre. In her 30's she discovered Allpoetry.com and has written there ever since. She loves to write books, has podcasts and even made audiobooks. She wrote Vivienne and the reaper her tale of life, love and death as a collections of poems for Allpoetry contests and added them together into one collected short story.

Rachel is a poet-writer versed in prose as much as she is rhyme. She loves to weave words and for the most part has no idea where the words are leading her to, she finds it the fun way to write.

In author's words on her writing style from her poem The Flow of Magical Words.

"I love words, which pour easily from my pen,

when I put pen to paper a world of words does open,

it flows on the page it's soul mate,

though no one can read the scrawl of words which well inside and opens a gate,

out comes beauty, rhymes of passion, sage words and gloom,

rhyming poem, deathly prose dark as the hand of doom,

the right word is magic in my hand,

like a lover sigh lightly fanned."

Videos are readings of her poems.

Rachel's poems are on google play music and iTunes music also on amazon digital music in audio and Kobo too. Rachel is also webmaster to her own poetry website rachellawsonpoet.yolasite.com/ contact her via email there.

Rachel is a distant relative and big fan of the famous but little know writer Fanny Burney who wrote Evelina who inspired Jane Austin. To learn of her google her name to find her book look on amazon she's every where.

Read more at https://rachellawsonpoet.yolasite.com/.

www.ingramcontent.com/pod-product-compliance
Lightning Source LLC
Chambersburg PA
CBHW031448130726
47989CB00003B/1311